AGAINST THE ODDS

Malala Yousafzai

Claire Throp

raintree
a Capstone company — publishers for children

Raintree is an imprint of Capstone Global Library Limited, a company incorporated in England and Wales having its registered office at 7 Pilgrim Street, London EC4V 6LB – Registered company number: 6695582

www.raintreepublishers.co.uk
myorders@raintreepublishers.co.uk

Edited by Linda Staniford and Jennifer Besel
Designed by Philippa Jenkins and Tim Bond
Picture research by Tracy Cummins
Production by Helen McCreath
Illustrated by Oxford Designers and Illustrators
Original illustrations © Capstone Global Library Limited 2015
Originated by Capstone Global Library Limited
Printed and bound in China by LEO

ISBN 978 1 406 29752 2
19 18 17 16 15
10 9 8 7 6 5 4 3 2 1

British Library Cataloguing in Publication Data
A full catalogue record for this book is available from the British Library.

Acknowledgements
We would like to thank the following for permission to reproduce photographs: Alamy: epa european pressphoto agency b.v., 37, LatitudeStock, 7; AP Photo: Alastair Grant, 23, Anja Niedringhaus, 20, Queen Elizabeth Hospital, 25; Capstone Press: HL Studios, 6; Corbis: BILAWAL, ARBAB/epa, 31, REUTERS/Gary Cameron, 35, REUTERS/Hoda Emam, 12, REUTERS/Russell Cheyne, 36 Xinhua/ISPR, 21; Getty Images: AAMIR QURESHI/AFP, 22, AFP PHOTO/ PATRICK HERTZOG, 38, Anadolu Agency, 40, Christopher Furlong, 5, John Moore, 9, KARIM SAHIB/AFP, 11, Mike Coppola/for Pencils of Promise, 30, Nigel Waldron, 41, Queen Elizabeth Hospital Birmingham, 27, 28, Robert Harding, 13, STAN HONDA/AFP, 14, Veronique de Viguerie, 16, 17, 19; Landov: EPA/MALALA PRESS OFFICE, 29; Newscom: Anthony Behar/Sipa USA, 43, EPA/JAMAL NASRALLAH, 39, HRC WENN Photos, 32, Pete Souza/Polaris, 34 Robin Utrecht/Sipa USA, 33; Shutterstock: CS Stock, Design Element; Thinkstock: Andrew Burton, 8, Andrew Burton, Cover.

We would like to thank the following for permission to reproduce quoted text:
pp5, 32, 33 ©Malala Yousafzai from speech given to the UN General Assembly, 12 July 2013; pp11, 27 taken from the book "I Am Malala" by Malala Yousafzai with Christina Lamb (Weidenfeld & Nicholson Ltd, Orion Books, 2013); p29 Reproduced by kind permission of The Guardian newspaper who published "Malala Yousafzai on life in Britain: We have never seen women so free" article, 7 October 2013; p41 Reproduced by kind permission of The Guardian newspaper who published "Nobel peace prize winners say award is a boost for children's rights worldwide" article, 10 October 2013; p43 Reproduced by kind permission of BBC News who published "Malala: The girl who was shot for going to school" article, 7 October 2013

Contents

Some words are shown in bold, **like this**. You can find out what they mean by looking in the glossary.

Who is Malala Yousafzai?

Malala Yousafzai is the girl who spoke out about the difficulties girls face getting an education in Pakistan, the country where she was born and where she lived at the time. She put her life in danger for this. Her efforts were so heroic that she is now a Nobel Peace Prize winner.

Taliban rules

Life was difficult for many women in the Swat District where Malala was born. They had very little freedom, with rules about where they could go and with whom, and even what they should wear. A Muslim **fundamentalist** group called the **Taliban** (see pages 8–9) were powerful in the area and enforced these rules. In January 2009, they said that girls should not be allowed to go to school.

"I speak not for myself, but so those without a voice can be heard. Those who have fought for their rights. Their right to live in peace. Their right to be treated with dignity. Their right to **equality** of opportunity. Their right to be educated."

Malala Yousafzai speaking at the **United Nations** in New York, USA, 12 July 2013

THE PASHTUN PEOPLE

Malala and her family are Pashtuns. Pashtuns are a group of people who live in northwest Pakistan and southeast Afghanistan. They speak their own language, called Pashto. More Pashtun people live in Pakistan than Afghanistan. It is thought that Pashtuns moved to Pakistan at some time between the 13th and 16th centuries.

Becoming a target

Malala wasn't afraid to speak out. As a result of the attention that she gained, Malala became a target for the Taliban. When her family received threats from the Taliban, Malala started travelling to school by bus instead of walking. On 9 October, she was shot in the head by the Taliban on the way home from school. Amazingly, she survived.

Malala Yousafzai has worked hard to improve children's education around the world.

What is Pakistan like?

Pakistan is a country in southern Asia. Pakistan was created after World War II, in 1947, when the country of India was divided to provide Indian Muslims with a country of their own. At first, there were two parts: East and West. In 1971, the East split off and became Bangladesh. An area called Kashmir has caused problems between Pakistan and India ever since. Wars have been fought over which country the area belonged to.

This map shows the main cities and towns in Pakistan.

CHINA

N
W E
S

Mingora

SWAT
VALLEY

Peshawar

AFGHANISTAN

Islamabad
Rawalpindi

Zhob   Faisalabad   Lahore

Quetta

Multan

Nok Kundi   Bahawalpur

IRAN   PAKISTAN

Indus   Sukkur

INDIA

Gwadar   Ormara   Hyderabad
Karachi

Arabian Sea

Snow and water from the mountains and glaciers flow down to the Swat River.

Landscape

In the north and northwest of Pakistan, one of the world's highest mountain ranges can be found – the Karakoram Range. K2, the world's second highest mountain, is also in Pakistan. Baltoro Glacier, one of the world's longest glaciers (a very slow-moving river of ice), is also in Pakistan. There are areas of very flat land, such as the Indus plain in the east and the Balochistan plateau in the west.

Swat District, where Malala was born, is in the north of Pakistan close to the border with Afghanistan. Swat is a long, thin valley, with other smaller valleys branching off it. At one end is Spin Ghar, which means White Mountain. A mountain called Tor Ghar (Black Mountain) is at the opposite end of the valley.

PAKISTAN FACT FILE

- Country name: Islamic Republic of Pakistan
- Population: 196 million (2014)
- Capital city: Islamabad
- Main languages: Punjabi, Sindhi, English, Pashto, **Urdu**, Balochi
- Main religion: Islam

7

Religion

Islam is the second largest religion in the world and its followers are known as Muslims. Malala and her family are Muslims. Muslims believe in one god, called Allah. Allah sent men – known as prophets – to teach people how to live by his law. The final prophet was Muhammad. The Muslims' holy book is called the Qur'an and it is believed to be Allah's own words as revealed to Muhammad.

MUSLIMS IN PAKISTAN

Pakistan has the third largest number of Muslims of any country. Over 96 per cent of Pakistanis are Muslim.

Muslims worship at mosques like this one in Lahore, Pakistan.

Armed members of the Taliban can be seen on the streets in some areas of Pakistan.

Who are the Taliban?

In 1996, a group called the Taliban came to power in Afghanistan and then moved into northern Pakistan in 2007. The area where Malala lived has suffered a lot of fighting between the Taliban and Pakistani soldiers. In early 2009, the Pakistan government tried to get the Taliban to agree to stop fighting, but the agreement did not last long. Bomb blasts and shootings continue to take place. Thousands of people have been killed.

The Taliban are a Muslim fundamentalist group. This means that they believe in a very strict reading of the Qur'an and hold extreme views on many issues, such as women's role in life. Their aim is to replace Pakistan's current system of government with an Islamic state, based on Islamic law.

One of the beliefs held by the Taliban is that girls should not go to school. They think that educating girls goes against Islamic law. Taliban **militants** destroyed more than 150 schools in 2008 alone.

Politics

The head of Pakistan is the president, while the **prime minister** runs the government. Pakistan has been governed by politicians and at other times it has been run by the **military**. This has resulted in unstable situations. Since 2007, the government has fought against the Taliban, with little success.

Tradition

In Pakistan, women have long struggled for equality with men. There are many women's rights groups in Pakistan, but they are often targeted by militant groups such as the Taliban. The Pakistan government has been accused of not doing enough to protect the women.

> "I was a girl in a land where rifles are fired in celebration of a son, while daughters are hidden away behind a curtain, their role in life simply to prepare food and give birth to children."
>
> Malala in *I am Malala*

While Pakistani **traditions** do not usually allow women to mix freely or work, some women have achieved fame in **politics**. Benazir Bhutto was the first woman to lead a Muslim country in modern times.

Benazir Bhutto
(1953–2007)

Bhutto was born in Karachi, Pakistan. She studied in the United States and the United Kingdom. Her father led the Pakistan People's Party (PPP) but he was killed in 1979. Benazir took over the leadership of the PPP and became Pakistan's prime minister in 1988. In 1990, the government was dismissed because it was thought to be **corrupt**. In 1993, Bhutto was again voted into power but defeated three years later. Corruption charges were brought again and Bhutto and her husband were given prison sentences. To avoid prison, Bhutto went into **exile** in the United Kingdom and Dubai. Bhutto returned to Pakistan in 2007, but died in a bomb blast.

What was Malala's early childhood like?

Malala was born on 12 July 1997 in Mingora, Swat District, Pakistan. She was not born in hospital but at home with the help of a neighbour because her family did not have enough money to go to hospital.

Malala's father, Ziauddin, set up a school with a friend. Malala's family lived in a shack that had only two rooms, opposite the school. Later, they moved into rooms above the school itself. When she was young, Malala's mother, Tor Pekai, never worked and could not read or write. Despite this, Ziauddin discussed everything with her. This is unusual; many men in Pakistan would think that asking for the opinion of a woman was weak.

Who's who

Ziauddin Yousafzai
(born 1969)

Ziauddin was born in Pakistan. He was part of a large Pashtun family, with five sisters and a brother. Part of his passion for education comes from the fact that his father did not allow Ziauddin's sisters to go to school. Ziauddin believes that girls should be educated and women should be free to do as they wish, rather than be controlled by their fathers or husbands. He ran a school in Pakistan, teaching both girls and boys, and since his family's move to the United Kingdom, he has worked for the Pakistan **consulate** in Birmingham.

MALALAI OF MAIWAND

Malala is named after Malalai of Maiwand, an Afghan heroine. The Afghans, including the man Malalai was meant to marry, were fighting the British in 1880. She went to the battlefield to help the wounded, but when she saw the Afghans were losing, she joined the fight. Malalai was killed, but she is still remembered for her bravery.

The Butkara ruins in Swat Valley are thought to date from the 3rd century BC. Malala used to play hide and seek there.

Top of the class

Malala would wander around her father's school as soon as she could walk. At the age of three or four, she was put into classes for older children.

Malala was used to being top of the class by the age of seven. She was usually in competition with her best friend, Moniba. Then a new girl arrived – Malka-e-Noor – and she was the one who finished top in the end of year exams. Malala was shocked by this – only Moniba had ever beaten her before. Malala later claimed, "At home I cried and cried and had to be comforted by my mother."

Malala is seen here with her mother, father and brother, Atal.

> "I had the run of the school as my playground ... You could say I grew up in a school."
>
> Malala Yousafzai

Brothers

Malala has two brothers: Khushal, who is two years younger than Malala, and Atal, who was born five years later. Khushal was named after a warrior poet, Khushal Khan Khattak. Traditionally, a boy is seen as more important than a girl, so Malala's mother was thrilled to have a son. She wanted to buy a new cot for him, but Malala's father said that the old one was good enough for Malala, so they did not need to change it.

Malala and her brothers spent most of their time with their mother. Some of Malala's favourite times were when the family had guests round for dinner and her father would tell stories and read poems afterwards.

MALALA'S FAVOURITE BOOKS

When she was 10, Malala loved the *Twilight* books. She and her friend Moniba wanted to be vampires!

When did Malala first begin to speak out about education?

During 2007, the Taliban gained control in Swat Valley. In July, they began attacking government buildings, including girls' schools. They believed schools for girls went against Islamic teaching. Malala's school was not bombed, but there was constant fear that it would be.

EDUCATION IN PAKISTAN

In 2009, 68.6 per cent of boys in Pakistan (aged 15 or older) were able to read and write, but only 40.3 per cent of girls.

In Swat District, only a third of girls go to school.

By March 2009, after her public appearances and her BBC blog, Malala's life began to change as she became better known in Pakistan.

On 1 September 2008, Malala made her first public appearance at Peshawar in front of national press to **protest** against the Taliban attacking girls' schools in July. Her speech was called "How Dare the Taliban Take Away My Basic Right to an Education?". This appearance brought Malala to the attention of the Taliban.

The Taliban announced that all girls' schools in Swat Valley were to be shut from 15 January 2009. Malala's father was asked by BBC Urdu if he knew a pupil who could write a **blog** about life under Taliban rule. One girl offered to write it but her parents said no because they feared what the Taliban would do if they discovered the **identity** of the blogger.

Writing a blog

Malala took up the challenge. She wrote under the name Gul Makai, the heroine of a folk tale. It was not safe to reveal her identity. The first entry in Malala's diary appeared on the BBC Urdu website on 3 January 2009. She wrote about her everyday life, particularly the way in which the ban on girls going to school affected her. On 14 January, she states that she is in a "bad mood" because she may not be allowed to go to school after the winter holidays.

TV and film

Malala was becoming well known for her opinions on education for girls. She appeared on a popular Pakistani television programme in February 2009, one regularly watched by 25 million people. She used it to publicize her views on education and to say that she was not afraid of anyone.

During 2009–2010, two documentaries were made about her by Adam Ellick, a **journalist** from *The New York Times* newspaper. He spent six months with Malala and her family. Originally, Ellick had interviewed Ziauddin, hoping to find a family in Swat that was affected by the banning of girls' education to report on. In the end, Ziauddin suggested his family. Malala's mother did not take part in the films, however, because of Pakistani tradition. She did not talk to men outside the family.

Forced to leave Swat

Unfortunately, in May 2009, many people living in Swat had to leave as major fighting took place between the Taliban and the Pakistani military. Malala's father stayed separate from the rest of the family in Peshawar because he was seen as the main danger to the family. He and three other men from Swat organized protests to try to persuade the government to work harder to stop the fighting.

AN AWARD FOR MALALA

In December 2011, Malala won the Pakistan National Youth Peace Prize for supporting girls' education. They renamed it the National Malala Peace Prize in her honour.

Malala and the rest of her family moved four times over the next couple of months. They didn't return to Swat until August. Their schools and city had been badly damaged. Malala's school – Khushal Public School – did not reopen until August, but other schools took longer to open again.

When Malala won the National Youth Peace Prize, she also received 500,000 rupees (about £3,000).

What happened to Malala in October 2012?

On 9 October 2012, Malala had a Pakistan Studies exam. She was worried about it and had stayed up late studying. It went better than expected and she and Moniba stayed behind at school to chat. They then caught the bus to go home.

When the bus turned off the main road, it seemed quieter than usual. Then a man stepped in front of the bus and asked if it was the Khushal School bus. At the back of the bus, another man asked, "Who is Malala?" Her friends unintentionally gave her away by glancing at her. The man fired three bullets towards them.

Malala shot

The school bus driver drove to the hospital in Mingora as fast as he could. Malala and two of her friends had been shot. Kainat Riaz had been grazed by a bullet in her arm and Shazia Ramazan had been shot in her collarbone and hand. Malala, however, had been shot in the head, the bullet entering above her left eye. It only just missed her brain.

Malala was a student at the Khushal School for Girls in Mingora.

Malala was rushed to hospital after being shot by members of the Taliban.

A few hours after her treatment in Mingora, Malala was flown to a military hospital in Peshawar. Military surgeon Dr Junaid Khan monitored Malala and after a few hours noticed that her brain was beginning to swell. He recommended **surgery** to remove the bullet from her body. Ziauddin was not keen at first because he thought Khan looked too young. It was also very risky, with the possibility of damage to Malala's speech and the right side of her body.

Success

Surgeon Junaid Khan operated on Malala for three hours in the middle of the night, removing part of her skull to give her brain room to expand. The piece of bone was kept in the tissue of her stomach to preserve it so that it could be replaced at a later date.

The operation was successful. Dr Fiona Reynolds, one of the doctors who cared for Malala later, in the United Kingdom, said, "I've got no doubt that he saved her life. He's a hero."

People around the world were waiting to hear what had happened to Malala. Thousands protested against the terrible actions taken by the Taliban.

Dr Kayani works at the Queen Elizabeth Hospital. This is where Malala was taken after flying from Pakistan.

After the surgery

Two British doctors – Dr Fiona Reynolds and Dr Javid Kayani – who were in Pakistan helping to set up a liver transplant programme, came to see Malala. It was clear that Malala had been given life-saving surgery, but the hospital was not very modern. Dr Reynolds was particularly concerned. She recommended that certain changes be made immediately and that Malala should be moved to a better hospital in Rawalpindi.

Who's who

Dr Fiona Reynolds and Dr Javid Kayani

Dr Fiona Reynolds was born in Falkirk, Scotland. She has many years of experience working with sick children. She is an **intensive care** consultant in charge of a team of doctors and nurses in the intensive care unit at Birmingham Children's Hospital.

Dr Javid Kayani was born in Pakistan. He was made a consultant in Emergency Medicine in 1995. He works at Queen Elizabeth Hospital in Birmingham as deputy medical director. He helps to train international medical students.

Moved to the UK

Doctors in Peshawar refused to move Malala, but the next day it was clear that her health had worsened. The Taliban then admitted that they had shot Malala. Security around the hospital was increased, and doctors discussed how to help Malala recover properly. Hospitals from all over the world offered care. Eventually it was decided that she be flown to the United Kingdom for recovery.

On 15 October, Malala was taken to Queen Elizabeth Hospital in Birmingham. This was where Dr Kayani worked. Dr Reynolds worked at the nearby Birmingham Children's Hospital, but she visited Malala nearly every day. Dr Reynolds was responsible for Malala during the flight and the first 10 days of Malala's stay in the hospital because Malala's father decided to stay with the rest of the family in Pakistan. It was thought to be too dangerous to leave them alone. It then took some time for her family to be able to travel to the United Kingdom.

A HOSPITAL ON A PLANE

Malala was flown to the United Kingdom in a jet belonging to the United Arab Emirates ruling family. The plane had its own hospital on board.

Another operation

On 11 November, Malala had another operation. This one was to repair a facial nerve. This nerve was part of her body that controlled things like raising an eyebrow or smiling. It took 8.5 hours. The surgery was successful, but it took about three months before Malala could start moving the left side of her face again. She had to perform facial exercises every day.

Malala was soon able to sit up and read.
She also spent many hours playing Connect
4 with nurses and doctors until her parents
arrived in Birmingham.

Well-wishers

Malala received hundreds of gifts and letters from people around the world, including two shawls that had belonged to Benazir Bhutto, the first female prime minister of Pakistan and one of Malala's heroines (see page 11). Malala had cards and messages from celebrities, including Beyoncé and Angelina Jolie. She also received 8,000 cards from well-wishers. One was simply addressed to "The girl shot in the head, Birmingham". One writer even proposed marriage!

Many people wanted to visit Malala but few were allowed to. Gordon Brown, who was once British prime minister and was now UN Special **Envoy** for Global Education, visited and brought books for Malala to read. He told her that he had set up a **petition** under the name "I am Malala", with the aim of getting every child into education by 2015.

"She [Dorothy] had to overcome a lot of obstacles to get where she was going, and I thought if you want to achieve a goal, there will be hurdles in your way but you must continue."

Malala after reading *The Wonderful Wizard of Oz*, a book given to her by Gordon Brown while she was in hospital

A Malala web page

Queen Elizabeth Hospital set up a special web page to report on Malala's progress because so many people wanted to know how her recovery was going. They also started a **fund** for her. On the day of their final report about her health, nearly £10,000 had been raised for the fund.

Malala's family finally arrived in Birmingham on 25 October.

What happened after Malala left hospital?

On 3 January 2013, Malala was finally able to leave hospital. She recorded a video message thanking people for their prayers and telling everyone that she was getting better every day.

More operations

In February, Malala had more operations, including one to replace the bone cut from her skull. Instead of using the original bone, which had been sewn into her stomach tissue to keep it healthy, a titanium metal plate was used. There was a risk of infection if the bone was used. Malala asked to keep the bone after it was decided to use titanium instead. Malala also had a cochlear implant placed in her ear to improve her damaged hearing.

Malala thanked the nurses who had helped to look after her before she left Queen Elizabeth Hospital.

In March 2013, Malala started at Edgbaston High School for Girls in Birmingham.

Life in Birmingham

Ziauddin was given a job at the Pakistani consulate in Birmingham for three years so that he could stay in the United Kingdom without getting a **visa**. The family moved into a flat in the centre of Birmingham and later into a house. Malala went to school at Edgbaston High School in March. Adjusting to life in Britain was hard for Malala. The family are keeping up their Pashtun **culture**. Malala still wears a shawl over her head, for example.

"It was difficult to adjust to this new culture and this new society, especially for my mother, because we have never seen that women would be that much free ... in our country, if you want to go outside, you must go with a man – if even your five-year-old brother goes with you it's fine, but you must have someone else, a girl cannot go outside all alone."

Malala Yousafzai

How has Malala's life changed?

In November 2012, Malala, Shiza Shahid (see box below) and others set up the Malala Fund to help pay for education for girls in Pakistan and around the world. One focus of the Fund is to increase awareness of the difficulties faced by girls in many countries. Another is to link with business people to help girls have access to education. The first project involved sending 40 girls to school in Swat Valley, where Malala lived.

Shiza Shahid
(born 1989)

Shiza Shahid was born in Islamabad, the capital city of Pakistan. She helped other people from a young age, volunteering at a relief camp after an earthquake. At the age of 18, Shahid moved to the United States to attend Stanford University. While there, she saw a film about Malala trying to bring the world's attention to the lack of education for girls. She arranged a summer camp for Malala and 26 other girls. It was Shahid who took charge of media interest in Malala's life after the shooting.

The Nobel Peace Prize nomination

In March 2013, Malala was **nominated** for the Nobel Peace Prize. She was the youngest-ever person to be nominated. It showed that Malala was now seen as a respected international figure. She became one of the people that journalists went to for comments on any stories relating to education or girls' and women's rights.

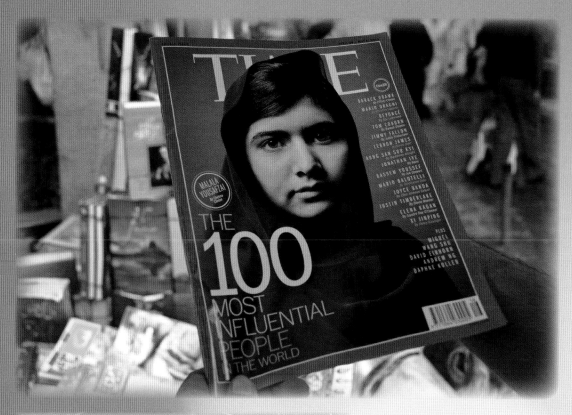

THE NOBEL PRIZE

Industrialist Alfred Nobel died in December 1896, leaving a will that said his fortune should be given out as prizes for outstanding achievements in Physics, Chemistry, Literature, Medicine and Peace. The Nobel Prize was first awarded in 1901.

Malala appeared in *Time* Magazine's top 100 most **influential** people in April 2013.

Malala spoke at the United Nations Youth Assembly in New York, USA in 2013.

"The wise saying, 'The pen is mightier than the sword.' It is true. The extremists are afraid of books and pens. The power of education frightens them. They are afraid of women. The power of the voice of women frightens them."

Malala Yousafzai

Birthday celebrations at the UN

On 12 July 2013, Malala spoke at the United Nations (UN). The UN is an organization that works to keep peace around the world. It was Malala's first time speaking in public since the shooting. It was also her 16th birthday. She called for free education for every child. The UN announced that 12 July would be known as Malala Day.

Malala wore a shawl that had once belonged to Benazir Bhutto. It was the shawl sent by Bhutto's children to Malala when she was in hospital. The event was also important because Malala's mother allowed herself to be photographed in public for the first time. Photographing women is not acceptable in much of **conservative**, traditional Pakistani society.

> "Dear brothers and sisters, do remember one thing: Malala Day is not my day. Today is the day of every woman, every boy and every girl who have raised their voice for their rights."
>
> Malala Yousafzai

International Children's Peace Prize

Malala won the International Children's Peace Prize in 2013, an award she was first nominated for in 2011. It was presented to her on 6 September 2013 in the Netherlands. In her acceptance speech, Malala pointed out that people in the Netherlands, the United Kingdom and many other places take going to school for granted – and that's how it should be. Malala announced that the prize money of 100,000 euros would be used to improve girls' education in Pakistan.

Malala received the International Children's Peace Prize in the Netherlands from Yemeni civil rights **activist** Tawakkul Karman.

What else did Malala do in 2013?

While many people around the world waited for news on the Nobel Peace Prize, Malala herself pointed out that winning the prize was not her main aim: "If I don't get it, it's not important because my goal is not to get Nobel Peace Prize, my goal is to get peace and my goal is to see education of every child."

Negative response

In the end, Malala did not win. Her friends in Pakistan had been sure she would win and were disappointed. However, other people in her hometown believed that Malala didn't deserve the prize. Some people thought that Malala was a spy for the West and others suggested she wasn't actually shot at all. Many people did not like her attempts to get girls educated. One worker in a bank said, "She doesn't deserve it [the Nobel Peace Prize] at all... Malala's interviews overseas will not help girls here." Some people thought that if Malala had won, more girls would have been hurt by the Taliban.

Malala met US President Barack Obama and his family at the White House during her trip to the United States in October 2013.

International Day of the Girl Child

Malala visited the United States in October 2013. International Day of the Girl Child was celebrated in Washington DC on 11 October. The day was created by the United Nations to bring attention to girls' rights and the challenges they face around the world, particularly in education. Malala spoke at the ceremony, telling her story and making a case for girls' education.

Malala attended the International Day of the Girl Child in Washington DC on 11 October 2013.

Global Citizenship Commission

On 19 October 2013, Malala joined Gordon Brown and many others at the first Global Citizenship Commission at the University of Edinburgh, Scotland. The Commission plans to update the Universal Declaration of **Human Rights** of 1948. This sets out the rights that all people should have, such as access to education. Malala gave a speech and then chatted to Gordon Brown in front of an audience of over 1,000. During the chat, she revealed that fighting with her brothers was a common event at home!

Who's who

Gordon Brown
(born 1951)

Gordon Brown was born in Glasgow, Scotland. At the young age of 16, he went to Edinburgh University and became very involved in politics. After he left university, he taught at Glasgow College of Technology and worked as a television journalist. In 1983, he became a Member of Parliament. He worked his way up to be prime minister from 2007 to 2010. In 2012, he was made the UN Special Envoy for Global Education.

Malala is seen here with Gordon Brown and Professor Timothy O'Shea at the first Global Citizenship Commission on 19 October 2013. She had been given an honorary degree, awarded for her support for girls' education.

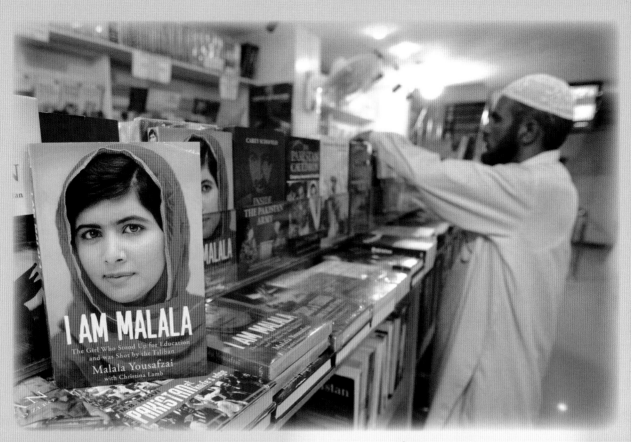

I am Malala

With help from American journalist Christina Lamb, Malala wrote a book called *I am Malala*. The book looks at her early life and examines in detail the events of October 2012.

Malala's book *I am Malala* went on sale in Pakistan's capital city, Islamabad, in October 2013.

Some private schools in Pakistan refused to have Malala's book in their libraries because they said its negative views of Pakistan would damage pupils' minds. The Taliban also threatened to attack any bookshops that stocked the book in Malala's home **province** of Khyber Pakhtunkhwa (KP). A book launch at Peshawar University was cancelled because of pressure from local government officials. It's thought that the Taliban forced the university to cancel the event.

Is Malala still making news?

There were more awards to come for Malala. In November 2013, she received the Sakharov Prize for Freedom of Thought, Europe's top human rights honour. It was presented to her by European Parliament President Martin Schulz, at a ceremony in France. The award is worth 50,000 euros, and is presented every year in memory of Russian scientist Andrei Sakharov, who won the Nobel Peace Prize in 1975.

Re-educating boys

Malala hasn't always been able to accept awards herself because she was at school. Malala's father accepted awards on her behalf. He was also asked to speak at other events, such as the Being a Man festival in London in January 2014. He suggested that re-educating boys to change their views on women was one way to help improve women's lives.

Malala gave a speech after receiving the Sakharov Prize at the European Parliament in November 2013.

Visiting the Zaatari refugee camp

On 18 February 2014, Malala and Shiza Shahid travelled to the Syria-Jordan border to stay at the Zaatari refugee camp for a week. This was a Malala Fund project to raise money for schools at the camp. Thousands of people who were forced from their homes because of war live there. The Fund plans to hire teachers and repair schools – one school for girls and one for boys.

There are only three schools at the camp for about 50,000 children. There are also cases where children have to work rather than go to school because they need to earn money for their family. Families are struggling because aid money raised by people around the world is not getting through. Malala and her father urged world leaders to visit the camp and see what was going on.

Malala spoke to the press while visiting the Zaatari camp in February 2014.

Nigeria

In April 2014, a militant Islamist group called Boko Haram **kidnapped** over 200 Nigerian girls. The group wanted to overthrow the Nigerian government and used bombs and kidnappings to try to achieve that aim. They said they planned to sell the girls. Malala got involved with the attempt to free the girls. She said that the girls were "my sisters" and that people should "not remain silent" about the kidnappings. She suggested that Boko Haram did not understand Islam. The faith encourages all people to be educated and to gain knowledge.

In July 2014, Malala visited Nigeria and met with some of the parents of the missing girls. She also tried to persuade the Nigerian president, Goodluck Jonathan, to meet with the families of the kidnapped girls. Eventually, on 22 July, the Nigerian government paid for a plane to take the parents and some of the girls who had escaped to meet the president in Abuja, Nigeria's capital city.

Malala met with the families of the kidnapped Nigerian girls to show her support.

The Nobel Prize committee described Malala and Kailash Satyarthi as "champions of peace". Malala and Kailash received their awards on 10 December 2014.

Nobel Peace Prize winner

The Nobel Peace Prize of 2014 was awarded jointly to Malala and Kailash Satyarthi, a man who fights for children's rights in India. The two winners agreed to work together to try to protect and educate children everywhere. They also hoped that the award would bring India and Pakistan closer together. Malala is the youngest-ever person to win the Prize.

"Through my story I want to tell children to speak for themselves, not to wait for someone else. I stand up with all the children and this award is especially for them. It will give them courage."

Malala Yousafzai

Malala's new life

From a young age, Malala has fought to bring attention to the issue of girls' education. She was targeted by the Taliban when her blog, her television appearances and her awards made her famous. Surviving being shot by the Taliban in October 2012 only made her an **inspiration** to even more people. Her speeches and actions have encouraged other well-known people to join in her fight. She has also inspired other young girls to stand up for their rights.

Returning to Pakistan

Malala's life has been turned upside down in recent years. She moved to a new and very different country from the one she was brought up in. Malala has said that she would like to return to Pakistan as soon as it is safe to do so.

In 2014, Malala won the Nobel Peace Prize, which she claimed was for "all the children whose voices are not being heard around the world".

In her book, *I am Malala*, she says that she does not want to be remembered for being shot by the Taliban. Malala wants to be remembered for standing up for the rights of girls everywhere. If the Taliban thought they could stop Malala by shooting her, they were wrong. She is now stronger and more powerful than before.

> "I think they [the Taliban] may be regretting that they shot Malala," she says. "Now she is heard in every corner of the world."
>
> Malala Yousafzai

Timeline

1997

Malala is born in Mingora, Swat Valley, Pakistan on 12 July

2007

The Taliban gain control in Swat Valley

2008

Malala makes her first speech at a protest against the Taliban in Peshawar, Pakistan

2009

Malala begins a blog for the BBC Urdu website, writing about the closing of schools and the right of girls to be educated

2011

Malala wins the Pakistan National Youth Peace Prize

2012

Malala is shot by the Taliban on her way to school on 9 October

2013

MARCH

Malala becomes the youngest-ever person to be nominated for the Nobel Peace Prize

Malala goes back to school on 19 March for the first time after the shooting. She attends Edgbaston High School for Girls in Birmingham.

JULY

Malala celebrates her 16th birthday by speaking at the United Nations in New York, USA, on 12 July

SEPTEMBER

Malala wins the International Children's Peace Prize

2014

FEBRUARY

Malala travels to the Syria-Jordan border to visit the Zaatari refugee camp for the Malala Fund

JULY

Malala visits Nigeria and meets President Goodluck Jonathan to discuss the Nigerian girls kidnapped by Boko Haram. She also meets with some of the girls' families.

OCTOBER

Malala is the joint winner of the Nobel Peace Prize

Glossary

activist person who works hard to bring an issue or subject to people's attention. This might be through demonstrations, for example.

blog website on which a person regularly writes their news and ideas

conservative having very traditional ideas and beliefs

consulate place where a consul works. A consul is a person who lives in a foreign city and protects the interests of people from his or her own country who live in that city.

corrupt dishonest; often refers to actions taken by people in government or business

culture ideas, customs and beliefs of a particular group of people

envoy representative of government

equality when everyone has access to the same things, such as freedom or education

exile when a person is unable to live in his or her own country

fund money to be spent on a particular project

fundamentalist person who believes in a very strict version of a religion

human rights things that many societies believe everyone should have, for example freedom, shelter, food and education

identity who somebody is

influential having an effect on someone or a group of people

inspiration something or someone that creates a positive feeling in people, encouraging them to do something

intensive care medical treatment for a person who is seriously ill or hurt. It involves the person being constantly watched over by doctors and nurses.

journalist person who writes about the news or who makes films about the news

kidnap take someone by force and ask for something, usually money, before the person will be released

militant person who uses violence to support something he or she believes in

military armed forces, such as the army

nominate put forward a person's name to win an award

petition appeal on behalf of a particular cause, often signed by many people

politics how a country or area is ruled. It usually involves different political parties, or groups of people who have similar ideas and beliefs.

prime minister head of government of a country

protest take action to show disapproval of something

province area of a country with its own local government

surgery treatment of injuries or diseases through operations carried out by surgeons

Taliban extreme Muslim group that wants to set up an Islamic state in Afghanistan and Pakistan

tradition passing on customs or beliefs to the next generation in a family or community

United Nations international organization set up to try to keep peace around the world

Urdu official language of Pakistan

visa document required for people from many foreign countries to live in other countries

Find out more

Books

I am Malala: The Girl who Stood up for Education and was Shot by the Taliban, Malala Yousafzai with Christina Lamb (Weidenfeld & Nicolson, 2014)

Malala: The Girl who Stood Up for Education and Changed the World, Malala Yousafzai with Patricia McCormick (Indigo, 2014)

Malala Yousafzai (Inspirational Lives), Claudia Martin (Wayland, 2015)

Websites

www.freethechildren.com
This is the website for one of the charities that Malala supports.

www.malala.org
This is the website for the Malala Fund.

poy.time.com/2012/12/19/interactive-timeline-malala-yousafzai
This website has a timeline of Malala's life up to the end of 2012.

Further research

- Try to find out more about the history of Pakistan, particularly the area where Malala was born.

- Learn as much as you can about Islam. What are the Five Pillars?

- What does the Malala Fund do? Research other groups that aim to help empower girls around the world.

- See if you can find out more about the different awards that Malala has won.

Index